Fiona the Theater Mouse

Study Guide

prepared by
Sheila Murray-Nellis

Eva Nova Press
P.O. Box 313
Kaslo, BC
V0G 1M0
Canada

ISBN 978-0-9691917-6-6

Contents

Theater Words

L	I	N	E	S	B	R	Y	A	L	P	C	A
M	A	W	F	T	R	A	D	G	U	I	I	A
R	C	N	L	A	A	S	N	C	K	A	S	R
E	A	O	M	E	L	P	A	U	E	N	U	O
D	R	E	S	S	I	N	G	R	O	O	M	N
A	L	M	T	T	L	R	B	T	G	B	A	R
N	A	I	A	E	U	S	O	A	N	S	E	A
C	M	P	G	J	K	M	B	I	E	P	L	F
E	D	A	E	H	U	A	E	N	R	O	E	T
S	I	T	C	L	T	D	J	S	B	R	N	E
S	T	S	O	N	G	S	E	B	A	P	N	R
W	B	A	L	C	O	N	Y	T	S	O	P	S

dressing room
curtains
stage
seats
post

lobby
piano
rafters
play

costumes
lights
balcony
music

props
lines
songs
dances

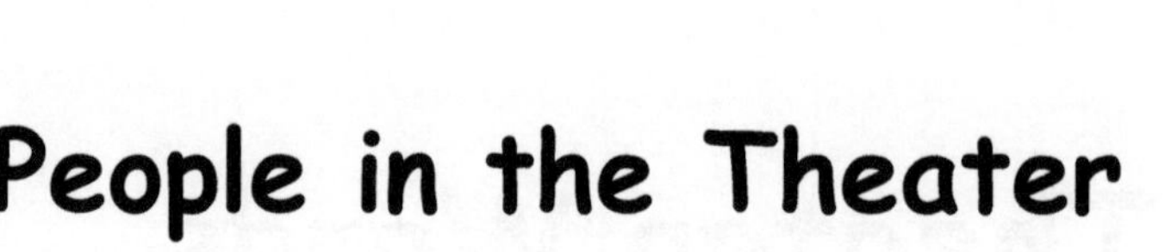

People in the Theater

Find out who else is in the audience! (Is your name there?)
Use this empty space to draw one of the people in the theater.

choreographer
audience
actors
janitor
director

singers
dancers
orchestra
ushers
concession

costume designer
stage manager
lighting director
mice
bat

B A P N A H T A N O J A L I L
C H O R E O G R A P H E R C I
M D F L N S A H U C T O M S G
M I C E O I I W D G T S V R H
V R D A I N L Y I E A O J E T
S E B A S G U B E K M P R H I
R C T R S E J A N I T O R S N
E T R O E R F T C M D P B U G
C O A N C S G O E J A K E L D
N R B A N K E N I L O R A C I
A M F I O N A K C I R T A P R
D L O R C H E S T R A D F W E
R E N G I S E D E M U T S O C
S T A G E M A N A G E R D L T
N A D N E R B N I L T I A C O
M A E L E N N Y O U N S A W R

Characters in the Story

Ma Mouse	Tommy	Bart	Margie	
Wilson	Donna	Marcy	Andrew	
Fiona	Jean	Charlie	Jane	Jeff

K	U	E	J	U	B	H	G	R	D	M
W	C	P	A	N	D	R	E	W	S	A
T	I	O	N	S	P	A	I	C	L	E
N	N	A	E	J	F	L	L	E	Y	L
F	O	M	N	Y	S	U	R	T	M	E
R	S	I	B	O	T	R	A	B	M	N
S	D	Q	N	W	I	S	H	D	O	N
E	B	H	F	M	V	F	C	U	T	P
Y	R	T	F	B	A	N	N	O	D	L
I	L	M	E	I	G	R	A	M	F	I
N	P	O	J	P	N	T	C	A	G	L
M	A	M	O	U	S	E	S	Y	R	A

Food

popcorn	sandwiches	seeds	olives	rice	pie
kernels	mosquitoes	flies	lentils	squash	ham
salami	breadcrumbs	moths	cereal	beans	tuna
crusts	peanut butter	milk	pizza	soup	
cheese	raisins	nuts	peas	tomato	

L	I	L	A	B	A	M	A	E	L	E	N	N	P
E	P	A	T	S	D	S	T	S	U	R	C	E	M
T	S	B	H	S	E	L	S	P	A	T	F	L	O
S	O	E	R	M	P	H	R	I	M	A	L	A	S
R	U	M	E	A	O	T	C	I	F	P	I	E	Q
A	P	R	A	H	P	T	L	I	C	B	E	R	U
I	L	D	B	T	C	K	H	S	W	E	S	E	I
S	E	V	I	L	O	R	S	S	N	D	A	C	T
I	N	A	K	E	R	N	E	L	S	A	N	P	O
N	T	S	T	U	N	P	E	A	S	R	E	A	E
S	I	P	B	R	E	A	D	C	R	U	M	B	S
E	L	H	S	A	U	Q	S	E	P	I	Z	Z	A
M	S	R	E	T	T	U	B	T	U	N	A	E	P

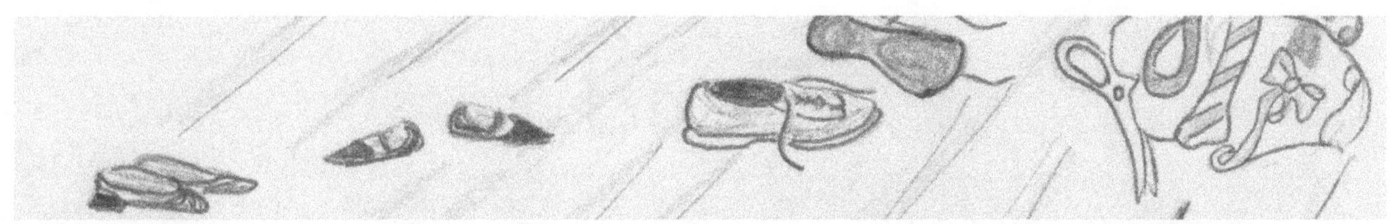

Things in the Dressing Room Closet

H S E O H S P B D A H M
A S R E H T A E F P I O
N E T I E A N M I C G U
G S E G B H T L E B H S
E S K M O B S U N K H E
R E C H R L O P Y L E F
S R A S I Y B N U Q E A
E D J E R I N U S R L M
A T R A P O K B A W S I
S P A R C S H T O L C L
D O O R T E R B O W S Y
M A E L E N N P A L I L

ribbons, dresses, shoes, mouse family, trap
feathers, pants, high heels, belt, jacket, tie
bows, mice, cloth scraps, door, hangers, hats

Discussion Questions

Chapter 1

1. Why do you think Ma told Fiona not to go onto the stage?
2. Why did Fiona go on stage anyway?
3. What dangers did Fiona face because she didn't listen to her mother? How did she put her family in danger?

Chapter 2

1. Why do you think Bart asked Fiona why she didn't have wings?
2. Have you ever had a friend who was different from you before? Can you imagine what it would be like to be without something you take for granted?
3. Why was Fiona so afraid while flying on Bart's back?

Chapter 3

1. Why was Ma upset when Fiona came back to the nest?
2. What was happening in the nest while Ma was talking to Fiona?

Chapter 4

1. Have you ever had trouble getting to sleep like Fiona? What did you do?

2. Have you ever had to do something you were afraid to do, the way Fiona had to climb the curtain? Did somebody help you?

Chapter 5

1. How were Fiona and Bart in danger?
2. Describe the conversation between the director and the janitor. Fiona could only hear a few words, but what do you think they were talking about?
3. What did the actors think they saw on stage, and how do you think they felt about it?

Chapter 6

1. Why did Ma tell Fiona to look for Bart?
2. How did Fiona help Bart?
3. Have you ever helped a friend in trouble? What did you do?
4. Can you think of another story in which a mouse helped a friend?

Chapter 7

1. Why do you think the hole Bart was resting in seemed familiar to him?

2. Bart wondered why Fiona had risked her life to save him. Why do you think she did it?
3. Do you know any other stories in which someone risked his or her own life to help someone else?

Chapter 8

1. What is your favorite kind of sandwich?
2. How do you think Ma and Fiona's brothers and sisters were feeling inside the mouse hole?
3. What did Fiona see when she went back to the stage? Why?

Chapter 9

1. When the actors opened the back door to get some air, what happened?
2. Why didn't Fiona go outside with Bart?
3. How did Fiona and Bart work together to save Fiona's family?

Chapter 10

1. Describe what happened after the mice left the mouse hole. What do you think the actors in the dressing room and on stage were thinking?
2. Pretend you were in the audience. Describe what you saw happening.

3. What do you think the mouse family found when they went outside?

Write another chapter to the book. What do you think happened after Bart and the mouse family left the theater? After you have finished your chapter, make a drawing to introduce your chapter.

Verb Match

(The words on the right are found in the chapter listed. If the word is a verb, or action word, it may appear in the past tense in the story. The description on the left is a loose definition of the word. If a word is new to you, you can figure out its meaning from the context or by looking it up in the dictionary.)

Chapter 1

Draw a line connecting the description on the left with the word on the right that most closely resembles it.

1. Spread	forage
2. Look with love/stare	bump
3. Follow someone's instructions	squeeze
4. Knock against	smear
5. Argue	twirl
6. Search for food	obey
7. Say something quietly	bicker
8. Jump into the air	whisper
9. Go around in a circle	leap
10. Make something smaller by pressing	gaze

Chapter 2:

Draw a line connecting the description on the left with the word on the right that most closely resembles it.

1. Laugh	squeak
2. Squish up	crash
3. Make a tiny, high pitched sound	squirm
4. Fix	tumble
5. Run (or fly) into	giggle
6. Move around obstacles	adjust
7. Move around uncomfortably with small movements	maneuver
8. Fall	wrinkle

Chapter 3

Draw a line connecting the description on the left with the word on the right that most closely resembles it.

1. Rub with your tongue	nip
2. Take a little bite	complain
3. Push someone a little	demand
4. Express unhappiness	scramble
5. Fight	nudge
6. Ask, expecting an answer	squabble
7. Mix up	lick

Chapter 4

Draw a line connecting the description on the left with the word on the right that most closely resembles it.

1. Shake slightly due to cold or fear	burst
2. Explode or push through	wrap
3. Make a little noise (as in the sound a door makes)	cling
4. Put around	perch
5. Pull with force	shriek
6. Hold on tightly	creak
7. Throw off with force	tiptoe
8. Sit on an edge	shiver
9. Scream	yank
10. Walk on your toes	fling

Chapter 5

Draw a line connecting the description on the left with the word on the right that most closely resembles it.

1. Cry quietly	
2. Move quickly	scurry
3. Shake with fear	holler
4. Look closely	examine
5. Laugh	chuckle
6. Get mixed up	startle
7. Try to stop	whimper
8. Surprise	tangle
9. Yell	suppress
	tremble

Math Fun

Depending on the age of the children, you may want to use manipulatives with some of these problems. They may be better to do as a collaborative activity, too.

1. If Ma and her seven baby mice can each eat three pieces of popcorn per night, how many pieces of popcorn do they need to find for all of them to have full bellies in one night? in one week? in one month*? in one year?

*Use your birthday month and compare your answer with the answers of your friends. Don't forget the rhyme:

30 days has September,
April, June, and November
All the rest have 31,
Except February, which has 28
And 29 when leap year's on.

2. The mouse family is getting ready for a nap. Ma Mouse lies down and all the baby mice are lined up in a row beneath her.
Andrew sleeps beside Jeff. Jeff is not beside Jean. Jane is between the littlest mouse and the biggest mouse. Fiona sleeps at the end and is not beside Jean. Charlie is the biggest mouse. Jean is next to the mouse who is beside the littlest mouse. Tommy is beside the biggest mouse and is not beside Jane. (Neither Andrew nor Tommy is the littlest mouse.*)
In what order is each mouse sleeping?

*Extra information if children are having trouble with this problem, though the answer can be figured out without it. Try leaving this bit of information out at first, and only add it if students find the problem too difficult, even with manipulatives.

3. If theater tickets cost $10.00 for adults and $5.00 for children under twelve, how much would it cost for a family with a mother and a father and two kids to see a play?
How much would it cost for a mother and her three kids to attend?
If Mr. O'Brien has $42.00 in his pocket, and wants to bring his four kids with him to see the play, how many boxes of popcorn can he buy and how much money will he have left over? (At this theater, a box of popcorn costs $2.50 each.)

4. If rehearsals begin on March 12, and the first performance is scheduled for May 4, how long do the actors have to rehearse?

5. If there are 23 rows of seats and each row has 18 seats, how many people can fit in the audience?

Would You Like to Take a Mouse to Dinner?
Or Maybe Even Have a Dinner of Mouse?

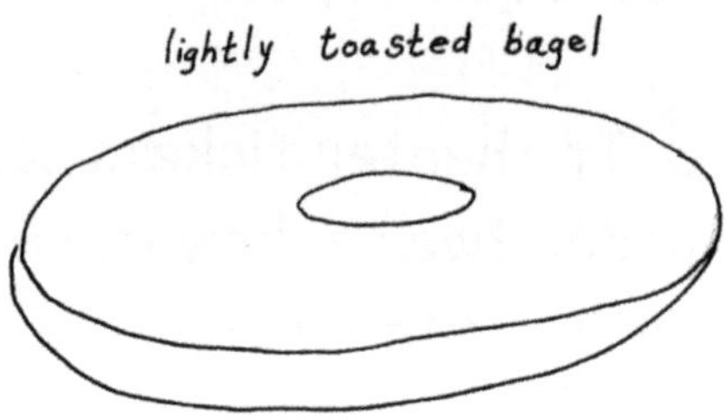

Cheesy Mice

Ingredients:

Sliced bagels
Apple slices
Apple wedges
Raisins
Grated cheddar cheese
Carrot sticks

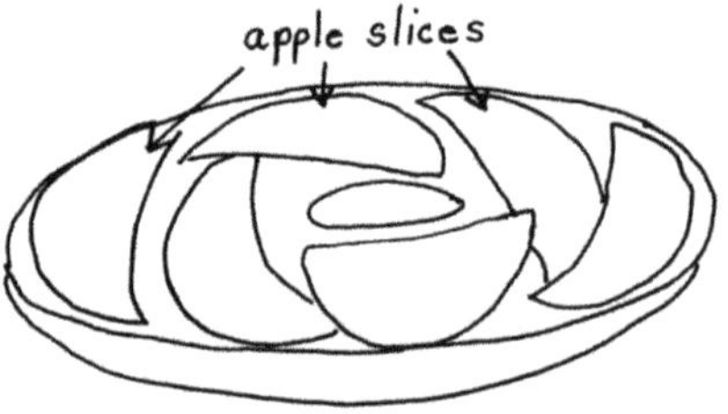

On each bagel slice, arrange apple slices.
Cover with grated cheddar cheese.
Bake in 350F oven until cheese melts.

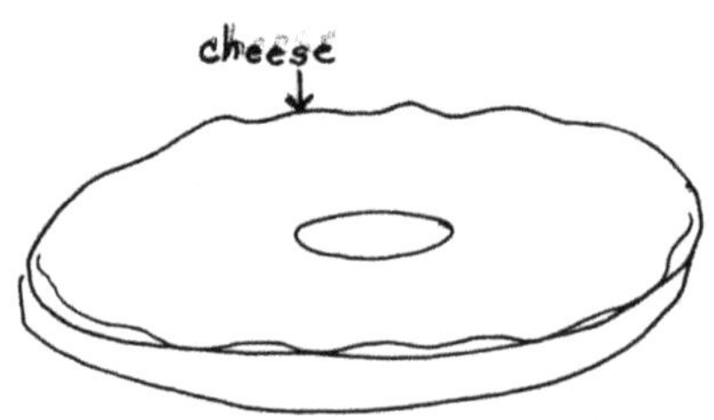

Decorate each apple cheese bagel to look like a mouse by adding apple wedges for ears, raisins for eyes and nose, and carrot sticks for whiskers.

Gobble it up!

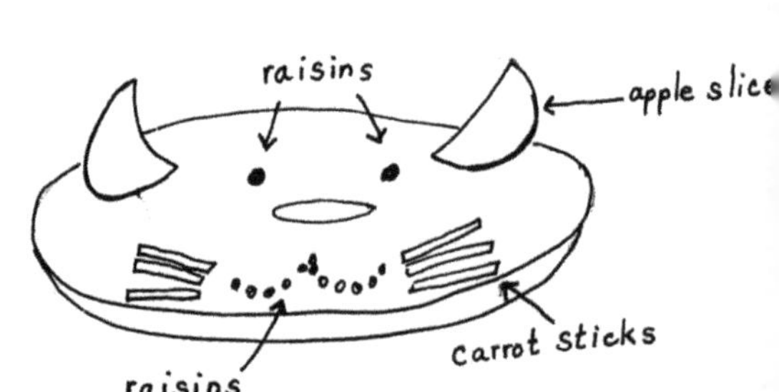

Avocado Mouse
(Or a "Pear" of Mice)

Ingredients for two mice:

1 avocado
1/2 lemon
1 small carrot, grated
4 whole cloves
4 almonds
Lettuce
Small wedge of cheese
for each mouse

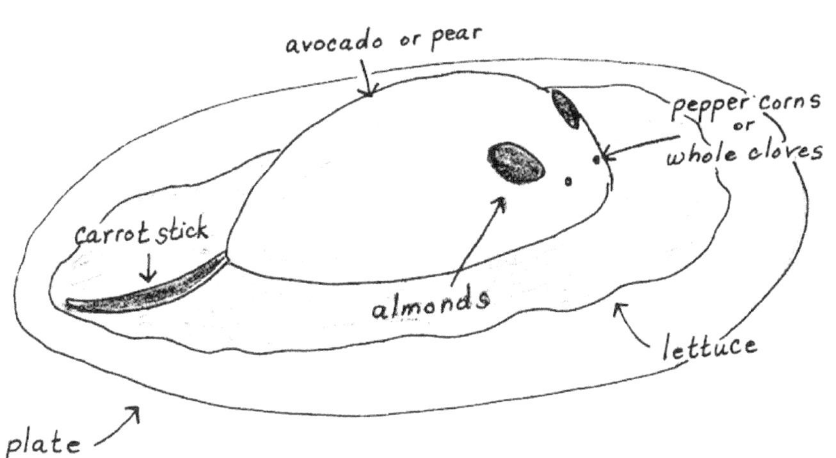

Procedure:

Cut the avocado in half lengthwise. Use a knife or spoon to slip off the peel. (This works best if the avocado is ripe.) Sprinkle with lemon juice to keep it from turning brown.

Put a lettuce leaf on each of two small plates. Arrange some grated carrot on top of the lettuce leaves.

Put 1/2 an avocado on top of the lettuce on each plate. This is your mouse body.

Place the almonds close to the smaller end of the avocado to look like ears.

Stick two cloves where the eyes would be.

Use a long piece of grated carrot for the tail, and place it on the plate on the larger side of the avocado. If you'd rather, you could cut a piece of the lemon peel to look like a tail and use it instead.

Place a small wedge of cheese in front of your avocado mouse.

Listen for squeaks.

(You can also make this mouse using half a canned pear in place of the avocado.)

No-Bake Chocolate Peanut Butter Mouse Cookies

Ingredients:

1 1/2 cups sugar
1/4 cup unsweetened cocoa powder
1/2 cup milk
1/4 cup margarine or butter
1 tsp vanilla
pinch salt
1/2 cup peanut butter

3 cups quick-cooking oats
1/2 cup raisins
1/2 cup chocolate chips (optional)

For decoration:

sliced almonds or peanut halves
a few raisins and chocolate chips
licorice string

Procedure:

In a medium-sized pot, mix together the sugar, cocoa, milk, and margarine. On the stove top, bring them to a boil, and let boil for one minute. Remove from heat.

Add the other ingredients (except for the nuts and a few raisins, chocolate chips, and licorice which will be used for decoration).

Drop the batter by teaspoonfuls on a sheet of waxed paper or parchment paper to look like little mice. Stick on two sliced almonds or peanut halves for ears and raisins or chocolate chips for eyes. If you don't have any nuts in the house, you can use raisins for both. Add a licorice tail. Let the cookies cool at room temperature.

Squeak when you nibble.

Mouse Cupcake Decorations

After you have iced your cupcake, place one of these decorations on top!

Terry, the cook at our local extended care facility, made a version of these to give out as Christmas presents last year. She put them on Oreo cookie halves and placed one by each person's setting at table on Christmas Day! So cute!

Ingredients:

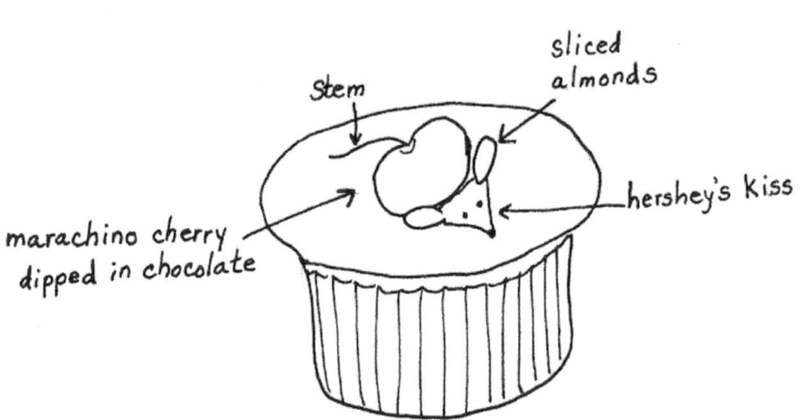

Maraschino cherries
Sliced almonds
Chocolate kisses

Procedure:

Melt a few chocolate kisses in a double boiler or in the microwave.
Take off the stove. Dip the maraschino cherries in the melted chocolate until covered. Remove and let cool on a plate. Arrange a chocolate kiss on its side on the cupcake. It should look like a mouse's head. Put the chocolate-dipped cherry close beside it to look like the mouse's body. Be sure the stem sticks out on the end for the tail. Using a little extra frosting as "glue," attach two sliced almonds on the head to look like ears. If you have any extra frosting, use a toothpick to apply eyes and a little nose.

Mouse Theater Diorama Directions

Cardboard box
Dowel or straight wire hanger
Fabric for curtain
Something to poke holes in the box (Caution: adults need to do this part!)

Choose a clean and sturdy cardboard box. A shoe box is a good choice, though you could use the kind of box that you get when you purchase items by mail. Make sure there are no flaps that will get in your way (though a cover would be helpful to close the theater up when you're not using it; don't worry if you don't have one, though, as a cover is totally optional).

Stand the box up horizontally on its side with the open side facing away from you and what is usually the bottom of the box facing in your direction. Cut a rectangular opening on the box's bottom about two inches in from the edges. Paint your box in whatever color you like using poster paints or tempera.

(Hint: You don't have to make the bottom of the box the opening for the stage, but if you do you'll have an easier time manipulating your puppets. You can add another curtain to the back of the stage to make a backdrop that you can still move past. You can also use the lid as a removable back wall that you can decorate with markers or fabric.).

On the sides of the box, poke a hole 1 inch down from the top and about an inch in from the surface from which you cut the rectangle.

Stick one end of the dowel into each hole and twist to make the hole big enough.

Cut a piece of cloth about one and a half times as long as the box and as high as the box plus two inches. For example, if my box is 12 inches long by 10 inches high, I will need a piece of cloth about 18 inches long and 12 inches high. Cut the cloth down the middle so that you have two curtains to draw across the stage. (In the example above, this would give you two pieces of cloth, each one measuring 9 inches x 12 inches.) Fold the top two inches of each cloth down and sew across to make a pocket for the dowel to fit through. (The curtains now measure 9 inches x 10 inches each.) Take the dowel out of its holes and push it through the two pieces of cloth. You can use bread bag twist ties to hold the curtains back.

How to Make Mouse Puppets

You have your choice as to how to decorate your stage and what kind of puppets to make. You can glue or tape pictures of mice to popsicle sticks for stick puppets for the easiest puppets, or you can make a sock puppet by adding felt ears and eyes to an old sock.

For something a little different, try the following idea.

Fur and magnet puppets

If you have some fake fur or even some cotton balls and some magnet tape, here's a fun idea for making mouse puppets.

If you are using fake fur, cut a piece about the size and shape of a mouse (a small oval).

If you are using cotton balls, dip the cotton balls into some brown tempera paint and let dry.

Cut a piece of shoelace for a tail.

Peel the backing from a piece of magnet tape cut the same length as the mouse. Put the end of the shoelace on the sticky side of the tape and the cotton ball or fake fur on top of that. Press firmly.

Place your mouse on the stage. Take a strong magnet and rub it underneath the cardboard to pull the mouse along the stage. With a little practice, you can get the mouse to move the way you want it to.

If you have some fake fur left over, use some of it for making a bat. Cut wings from light weight cardboard, paint them brown or black, and glue them to the fur oval you've cut about the same size as the piece you've used for the mouse. Make sure the wings are above and the body hangs underneath them. Attach a string to the bat and hang the bat by string from the ceiling of the stage.

One way to maneuver the bat is to poke a little hole in the roof and thread the string through. You can pull on the string to raise the bat up or let it down to lie on the stage. Unfortunately, this will not allow you any movement from side to side, but at least you can move it up and down. If you want it to go side to side, you may have to attach the bat to a longer dowel or even a piece of string that you can pull at from the side of the stage. This, of course, will require another hole in the stage wall.

Have fun putting on your puppet show!

Facts About Mice

Where can you find mice?

Mice really are everywhere! You can find varieties of mice in all corners of the globe and living in all climates. But mice are good at hiding. You may not see a mouse very often, but that doesn't mean there may not be mice living nearby.

Mice are rodents, just like rats and squirrels. What all rodents share is that they have sharp front teeth that never stop growing. Rodents are a sub-group of mammals, which means that a mother mouse gives birth to her babies and feeds them with milk from her mammary glands.

There are many different kinds of mice, some of which live in only a small area and others of which are spread across continents. North America is the home of hundreds of types of mice.

The mouse's closest cousin is the vole, which is often mistaken for a mouse. The vole is a little bigger than a mouse but has smaller eyes and ears and a shorter tail. Its common name is the field mouse.

The deer mouse is found all across the continent while more specialized mice, such as the Sitka mouse, can only be found on some of the smaller Haida Gwaii islands (formally called the Queen Charlotte Islands) off the west coast of Canada.

What do mice eat?

In general, mice are not picky eaters (even though Ma Mouse criticized the diet of bats). Depending on where they live and what kind of mice they are, mice will eat whatever they find close at hand. A deer mouse's favorite food is seeds, though deer mice may enjoy fresh buds and even new leaves in the spring time. A meadow vole finds grass very tasty, but will also eat roots and seeds and bark. Most mice also enjoy the occasional bug or caterpillar to round out their diet. And, of course, if a mouse lives in your house, you may find little nibbles on the bread bag or on your apples or frankly on any food item you may leave out or that they can get into!

What are mouse nests like?

Mice build their nests in hidden places. Outdoors a mouse nest can be in a hollow log, in an underground burrow, under rocks, or anywhere that feels private and safe. Inside a mouse may choose to build a nest inside the walls or in a hidden place in your basement. The nest itself is made with grasses, twigs, fur, cloth, string, yarn, or whatever the mouse finds handy. The mouse hollows out the inside and lines it with the softest material it can find -- moss, fur, or the down from thistles of milkweed or another plant.

How many babies does a mother mouse usually have?

Mice can begin to mate when they only three or four months old. The male and the female will share a nest for a few days and the babies are born three weeks later. Depending upon how well the mother has been eating and her age, a mother mouse can have a litter of five to seven babies, but could even have many more.

Newborn mice stay close to their mothers, nursing almost constantly for the first few days. At birth they are less than four centimeters (one and a half inches) long from head to tail. They have no fur and are blind and deaf. But after only four days or so, their fur has started to come in and after a week, they have doubled their birth weight. They can see at two weeks old.

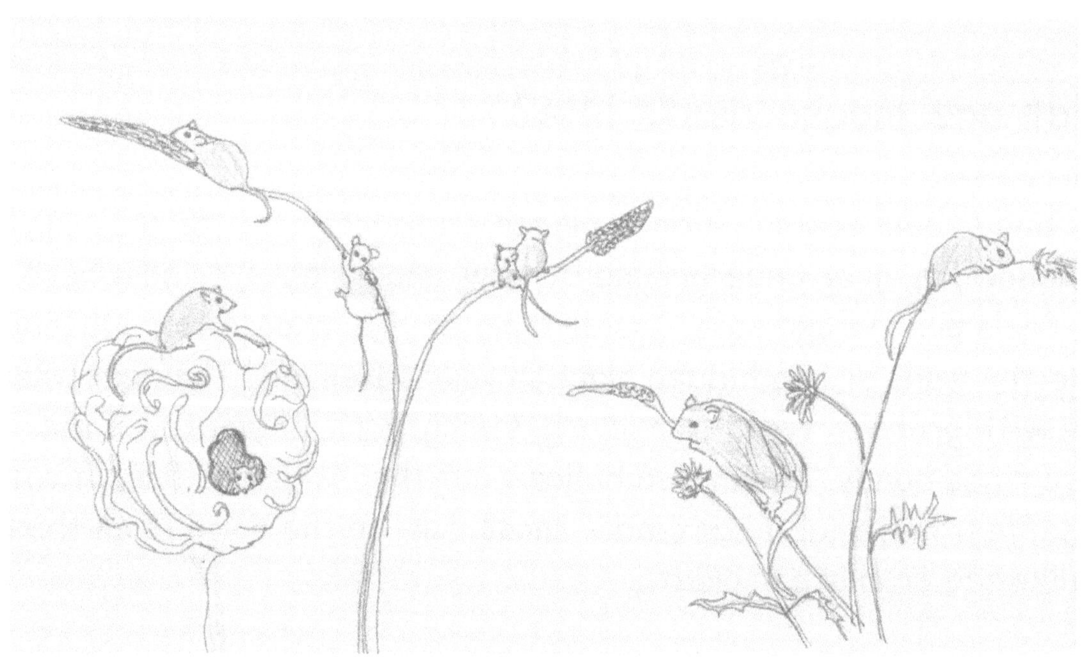

Some father mice help the mother take care of the little ones, keeping them warm and clean and teaching them how to find food. After a few weeks, the babies are all grown up and ready to strike out on their own.

How long do mice live?

Mice live for about a year and a half. This doesn't seem like a long time to us, but for a mouse, it's a lifetime!

Mouse Crossword Puzzle

Across:

1. Where can you find mice?
4. How many varieties of mice live in North America?
5. What part of a mouse's body keeps growing?
7. How many baby mice were in Ma Mouse's litter?
8. Favorite food of deer mice.

Down:

2. What animal is a mouse's closest cousin?
3. What kind of mammals are mice?
5. How many weeks after the parents mate are baby mice born?
6. Steaks for a mouse.
7. At two weeks old, a baby mouse can _____ for the first time.

1 2 3

4

5

6

7

8

Facts About Bats

A note about bats:

Bats are not really blind, though for a long time people thought they were. Bats do have eyes and, can see just fine during the day. However, unlike you and me, bats have to find their food in the dark, which is when they are active.

That's okay, though, because bats can hear better than other land mammals. They also have an ability to use that excellent hearing to help them find their food. Bats make very high pitched squeaks that bounce off objects, letting the bat know just how far away the object really is. It's similar to the echo you can hear when you yell near a rocky cliff or in an empty room. The difference is that a bat's hearing is so good that he can locate the distance of the object with no problem at all.

In the story, Fiona uses the phrase "blind as a bat." People sometimes say things like that, too, about other people. Often these sayings can really hurt other people's feelings. Not only that, but these words can be false, as well.

Where do you find bats?

Like mice, bats are rodents that can be found in most places of the world. Bats come out at dusk and return home in the morning. Although lots of bats live in caves, bats will also take up residence in barns or other places they can squeeze inside. Bats roost upside down in groups.

What do bats eat?

Depending on the type of bat and where they live, bats can eat many different types of food. In North America, most of our bats feast on mosquitoes, flies, moths, and other flying insects.

In tropical climates, such as in South America, bats often eat fruit (fruit bats). In fact, bats are responsible for spreading 95% of the seeds of fruit trees in the tropical rain forests.

Some bats even eat small mammals, and the so-called vampire bat is known for piercing the hides of large mammals, such as cows and horses, and lapping up the blood from the wound. Vampire bats aren't known to attack humans, however, and they don't turn into human vampires. That's just in stories. Vampire bats can be found in some tropical climates. They don't exist in North America.

What is echolocation?

As explained above, echolocation is the name given to the bat's ability to make rapid high pitched sounds that bounce off surfaces and return

to the bat's ear. The amount of time it takes for the sound to return helps the bat determine how far away the objects are.

Tell Me About Bat Babies!

Bat mothers usually have only one baby at a time, though they will sometimes have twins. Babies, called "pups," are born in the spring. They are small and pink and have no hair. They do have, however, very strong legs and claws because, to drink their mother's rich milk, they have to hold on tight to her while she is roosting upside down. They also need to hang onto the roost while she's away gobbling up bugs and mosquitoes.

Bat babies grow very fast. Some will be flying on their own and finding their own food when they are only a month old.

Bat Crossword Puzzle

Across:

3. What kind of animal is a bat or a cat?
4. When are bats active?
5. Another name for early evening when it's beginning to get dark
7. What is a newborn baby bat's food?
8. A favorite food of North American bats
11. What some bats in the tropics eat
12. What do you call a bat baby?
13. How many babies does a mother bat usually have?
15. Where bats sometimes live when there are no caves nearby

Down:

1. Baby bats are born with very strong _______.
2. The special ability bats have to measure distance
6. How bats roost
9. A verb that describes how bats fly
10. With echolocation, bats find out where things are by using high-pitched ________.
14. Bats sleep during the _____.

Bat Crossword Puzzle

Writing Activities

1. If Fiona started a newspaper, what kinds of stories do you think she would write? Imagine you are Fiona and you want to write a newspaper story about one of the events in the book. Some possibilities:

News
Fashion
Celebrity Watch
Editorials
Comics
Births
Obituaries
Classified
Arts
Sports
Travel

Choose at least one section and write a story from Fiona's viewpoint. Imagine the newspaper will be read by other mice. Don't forget to use vivid verbs in your writing!

If you are in a classroom, gather the stories of your classmates into a class newspaper. Brainstorm some possible titles for your newspaper.

2. Pretend you are Ma Mouse trying to protect your children as they venture out into the wide world. Write an advice column, in which you are trying to help the young ones find their way. You can do this as a how-to essay or as questions and answers (like "Dear Abbey" or "Ask Beth" from the past).

3. Do you think the theater was a good home for the mouse family or for a bat? Write a persuasive essay discussing your position. Begin by listing five to ten reasons why you feel the way you do. Write another five to ten reasons why someone may disagree with you. Then try to answer those disagreements. Finally write your essay.

4. Pretend you are Bart. Write a diary entry about your first meeting with Fiona. Write another diary entry after she saved you from the janitor. Finally write a diary entry after you led the Mouse Family outside, describing the event.

Answer Pages

Math Answers:

1. One night: 24 pieces.
One week: 168 pieces.
One month: 672 pieces (28 days); 696 pieces (29 days); 720 pieces (30 days); 744 pieces (31 days).
One year: 8,760 pieces.

2. Jean Andrew Jeff Jane Charlie Tommy Fiona

3. $30.00; $25.00;
Mr. O'Brien will spend $30.00 for tickets and can buy four boxes of popcorn. He will have $2.00 left over.

4. The actors have 53 days to rehearse.

5. 414 people.

Things in the Dressing Room Closet

```
H S E O H S P B D A H M
A S R E H T A E F P I O
N E T I E A N M I C G U
G S E G B H T L E B H S
E S K M O B S U N K H E
R E C H R L O P Y L E F
S R A S I Y B N U Q E A
E D J E R I N U S R L M
A T R A P O K B A W S I
S P A R C S H T O L C L
D O O R T E R B O W S Y
M A E L E N N P A L I L
```

Food

```
L I L A B A M A E L E N N P
E P A T S D S T S U R C E M
T S B H S E L S P A T F L O
S O E R M P H R I M A L A S
R U M E A O T C I F P I E Q
A P R A H P T L I C B E R U
I L D B T C K H S W E S E I
S E V I L O R S S N D A C T
I N A K E R N E L S A N P O
N T S T U N P E A S R E A E
S I P B R E A D C R U M B S
E L H S A U Q S E P I Z Z A
M S R E T T U B T U N A E P
```

Theater Words

```
L I N E S B R Y A L P C A
M A W F T R A D G U I I A
R C N L A A S N C K A S R
E A O M E L P A U E N U O
D R E S S I N G R O O M N
A L M T T L R B T G B A R
N A I A E U S O A N S E A
C M P G J K M B I E P L F
E D A E H U A E N R O E T
S I T C L T D J S B R N E
S T S O N G S E B A P N R
W B A L C O N Y T S O P S
```

Characters in the Story

```
K U E J U B H G R D M
W C P A N D R E W S A
T I O N S P A I C L E
N N A E J F L L E Y L
F O M N Y S U R T M E
R S I B O T R A B M N
S D Q N W I S H D O N
E B H F M V F C U T P
Y R T F B A N N O D L
I L M E I G R A M F I
N P O J P N T C A G L
M A M O U S E S Y R A
```

People in the Theater

B A P N A H T A N O J A L I L
C H O R E O G R A P H E R C I
M D F L N S A H U C T O M S G
M I C E O I I W D G T S V R H
V R D A I N L Y I E A O J E T
S E B A S G U B E K M P R H I
R C T R S E J A N I T O R S N
E T R O E R F T C M D P B U G
C O A N C S G O E J A K E L D
N R B A N K E N I L O R A C I
A M F I O N A K C I R T A P R
D L O R C H E S T R A D F W E
R E N G I S E D E M U T S O C
S T A G E M A N A G E R D L T
N A D N E R B N I L T I A C O
M A E L E N N Y O U N S A W R

Mouse Crossword Answers

Bat Crossword Answers

Verb Match

Chapter 1

1. smear
2. gaze
3. obey
4. bump
5. bicker
6. forage
7. whisper
8. leap
9. twirl
10. squeeze

Chapter 2

1. giggle
2. wrinkle
3. squeak
4. adjust
5. crash
6. maneuver
7. squirm
8. tumble

Chapter 3

1. lick
2. nip
3. nudge
4. complain
5. squabble
6. demand
7. scramble

Chapter 4

1. shiver
2. burst
3. creak
4. wrap
5. yank
6. cling
7. fling
8. perch
9. shriek
10. tiptoe

Chapter 5

1. whimper
2. scurry
3. tremble
4. examine
5. chuckle
6. tangle
7. suppress
8. startle
9. holler

www.ingramcontent.com/pod-product-compliance
Ingram Content Group UK Ltd.
Pitfield, Milton Keynes, MK11 3LW, UK
UKHW051134260726
13967UKWH00010B/3044

9 780969 191766